Books by Mari Sandoz published by
the University of Nebraska Press

The Battle of the Little Bighorn
The Beaver Men: Spearheads of Empire
The Buffalo Hunters: The Story of the Hide Men
Capital City
The Cattlemen: From the Rio Grande across the Far Marias
Cheyenne Autumn
The Christmas of the Phonograph Records
Crazy Horse: The Strange Man of the Oglalas
The Horsecatcher
Hostiles and Friendlies: Selected Short Writings of Mari Sandoz
Letters of Mari Sandoz
Love Song to the Plains
Miss Morissa: Doctor of the Gold Trail
Old Jules
Old Jules Country
Sandhill Sundays and Other Recollections
Slogum House
Son of the Gamblin' Man: The Youth of an Artist
The Story Catcher
These Were the Sioux
The Tom-Walker
Winter Thunder

THESE
WERE THE
SIOUX

by

MARI SANDOZ

UNIVERSITY OF NEBRASKA PRESS
LINCOLN AND LONDON

First Bison Book printing: 1985

Library of Congress Cataloging in Publication Data
Sandoz, Mari, 1896–1966.
    These were the Sioux.
    Reprint. Originally published: New York: Hastings
House, c1961.
    1. Dakota Indians. I. Title.
E99.D1S2 1985   923'.0497   85-8914
ISBN 0-8032-9151-5 (pbk.)

Reprinted by arrangement with the Estate of Mari Sandoz,
represented by McIntosh and Otis, Inc.

Contents

CONTENTS

A Note on the Illustrations and the Artists

Amos Bad Heart Bull, Oglala Sioux (nephew of He Dog, the brother-chieftan and friend of Crazy Horse), was the outstanding recorder of the Reno and Custer fights. He came from a long line of band historians, as honored as hunters and warriors. The histories were in pictures, the identification of individuals not by any physical resemblance but by the accouterments: shield, warbonnet, bead designs, and so on, although much of this probably was not worn in the scene depicted. Warrior and hunter usually worked stripped to breechcloth and moccasins.

Kills Two was also an Oglala but primarily an artist.

The drawings are from the portfolio "Sioux Indian Painting, Part II" published by Editions d'Art C. Szwedzicki. We are indebted to University of Nebraska Press for permission to reproduce those by Amos Bad Heart Bull.

FOREWORD

T HE SIOUX INDIANS CAME INTO MY LIFE BEFORE I had any preconceived notions about them, or about anyone else. In our family no formal pattern of philosophical or religious thought was thrust upon the children, and I was left free to learn about our Indian friends as I did about the rest of our neighborhood of mixed beliefs, languages and origins—homeseeking immigrant Poles, Czechs, Irish, Dutch, French, Germans, Danes, Swiss, a few Serbs, a Bulgar, a Mohammedan, a Negro and a smattering of so-called native Americans, including Texas cowboys.

To me the dress of the Indians was just another folk costume, their language no stranger than English to my German-Swiss ear. But there was something most engrossing about these Sioux and their tipis, their campfires, their drumming in the night and their ways with thunderstorms, small children and the mockingbird in our woodpile. And as I grew older I began to catch a glimpse now and then into the meaning of the customs and beliefs of these brown-faced people, a little like the view from a high mountain as the mist begins to break over the far plains.

MS

GOING TO THE WARRIORS' DANCE, in the later, the gun-armed days, incidentally showing a variety of costumes, including the breechcloth and moccasins usually worn in hunt and war.

THESE WERE THE SIOUX

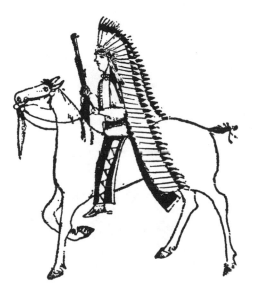

THE GO-ALONG ONES

THE FIRST INDIAN THAT I REMEMBER WAS FAR back in my childhood, soon after I learned to walk. I was very shy with people but apparently I had the toddler's daring and fondness for exploration. I liked to slip back to something I had been shown, perhaps a bird's nest in a thistle or the first brush roses. This day it was the wild plum thicket down the slope, with the fruit ripe and sweet, that tolled me from my grandmother's side. I recall some uneasiness about the wasps buzzing over the rotting fruit on the ground. Then something startled me—a face peering through the fall leaves. It was a brown face with dark eyes, and although there were braids like my grandmother's, and no such beard as my father wore, I knew this was a man.

The face was down at my level, the murmuring sounds of the man friendly and laughing, the hands reaching for me with no anger in them. I felt shy but I let myself be drawn out of the thicket, lifted high up on the man's shoulder, and given a braid for each hand, like reins. Then the man made the "Tchlch" sound that started horses, and prancing a little, but gently, he went up the slope toward our house, where there were more of these brown-faced people, a whole confusion of them, as I recall now—men, women with babies, some as large as I, on their backs, and many boys and girls running everywhere. Suddenly I became shy again, perhaps of all the people, and was clutching the man about the head with my arms so that everybody laughed. But my plump little old-country grandmother hurried up, as excited and alarmed as if I were being scalped. The man stooped so she could reach me. I cried, I am told, with fright, but as I was often reminded later, my fingers had to be pried out of the man's strong black braids—a little towheaded white girl clinging shamelessly to the hair of a bloodthirsty Sioux who had helped annihilate General Custer.

Later I discovered that Bad Arm, as the man was called because real names of Indians were seldom spoken, had received his lumpy elbow from an injury in the fight on the Little Big Horn with Crazy Horse. In 1890 at Wounded Knee, South Dakota, Custer's Seventh Cavalry got its revenge. Bad Arm had to see his wife and children shot down by the Hotchkiss guns after he had surrendered his old pistol.

Yet somehow this man could still be so gentle and playful with a small girl of the whites. Later I saw much of this amused and playful way of the Sioux with small children as the Indians came and went from their old camping ground near our house. They liked to return to the place that they said was already smooth and warm from long living when the tribe first reached the Niobrara country almost two hundred years before. They liked to visit our father, too. He had hunted deer with them before the settlers came. He still repaired their guns, gave them salves to heal the many sores that came with the starvation diet of the reservation and he made silver-nitrate solution for their trachomatous eyes.

These old buffalo-hunting Sioux of my early childhood spoke very little English and I knew only the German-Swiss dialect of my grandmother. But young children learn the rudiments of sign talk more quickly than any spoken language, perhaps because it usually tells a story and is so descriptive, so amusing. The extended right hand held before the chest, palm inward, and moved to the left in a sinuous path was the simplified sign for *fish*; with only the index finger extended, like an inquiring head pushed forward, the curving motions made larger, it was a snake. To tell of the hunts the partly closed hands might be brought up to each side of the head and tilted forward a little, like curved horns, for *buffalo*. This, preceded by the thumb pointing back to the sign talker himself, and followed by the nearly closed right hand brought downward from the shoulder in the swift gesture of destruction said, all together, "I buffalo killed." Fingers held up added their numerical information: "I two buffalo killed," and so on.

The Indians made names for us children in their teasing way. Because our very busy mother kept my hair cut short, like my brothers', they called me Short-Furred One, pointing to their hair and making the sign for short, the right hand with fingers pressed close together, held upward, back out, at the height intended. With me this was about two feet tall, the Indians laughing gently at my abashed face. I am told that I was given a pair of small moccasins that first time, to clear up my unhappiness at being picked out from the dusk behind the fire and my two unhappy shortcomings made conspicuous.

When I was about five or six I saw another kind of medicine, a bit of magical Sioux rite. I was very much afraid of electrical storms, perhaps because our father, despite his training in science and his acknowledged fearlessness before a grizzly bear or a hired gunman, was terrified of lightning. In the violent summer storms of the Great Plains he ordered everybody under the feather ticks, considered lightning proof.

One Sunday I sneaked away to watch the Indians spill out of several wagons and hurry to throw up their old canvas tipis before the great piling thunderhead that bent over us broke into rain from that flashing and roar. At an earth-shaking bolt of lightning and a shout from the house I turned to run home, but I was stopped by the sight of an old Indian coming out of one of the tipis walking on his moccasined hands, his bare toes gesturing in the air like blunt, appealing fingers above odd noises that seemed words spoken backward. Slowly he circled on the worn campground as though in stately ceremonial march while some of the Indians laughed and sang to him. Everything about the man seemed upside down and backward; even what had looked like his face was a mask of some sort, with the big nose pointing in the opposite direction from his toes. I think I laughed, too, my fear forgotten until I was yanked away by the collar of my dress and whipped soundly for disobedience.

By the time I finished my short crying, the dry storm was gone, blown away. The Indian women had their blackened coffeepot on the fire for the man who, I discovered years later, was a *heyoka*, a Contrary. He was one of those who had dreamed of thunder in his puberty fasting and to avoid this threat of lightning for himself, and for those about him, he must do all things in an unexpected, backward and foolish way, like the walking upside down, with the false face behind. The *heyoka* often dipped his supper out of the boiling kettle with his bare hands (perhaps coated with a secret preparation from resinous plants) and rode his horse facing the tail, his bow or gun drawn against himself. And if a man giving himself pompous airs around the camp or village should hear laughing behind him he could guess that a Contrary was there, imitating him, but in reverse, turning all the sweetness of the man's self-importance to sand in the teeth.

The Contrary not only tried to protect himself and those around him from lightning and other storm damage with his foolishness, he entertained the people as a clown entertains. With his antics he lifted the hearts that were on the ground, perhaps from some great dying brought by the white man's diseases or in the sorrow of another great loss, as when many were killed in a buffalo stampede or in warring, and when the homes of the people, their beloved hunting grounds, were taken away. This double purpose of the Contrary's dream seems typically Sioux. To them all the destructive aspects of nature were matched by the good, the wholesome, the creative. Storms that scattered the camps, drowned the people and the earth's creatures, or froze them, also made the grasses grow, the buffalo fat, the people full and contented. The lightning that might kill a whole war party or a dozen people from a traveling village on a high ridge somewhere could also reveal enemies skulking in the night and save the camp. Since the reservation days there was danger from lightning in the wagons with iron tires. But the Contraries worked hard, and through their antics brought a feeling of safety, with a little laughter and gaiety even in these defeated times. And when the storm clouds broke away, there was sometimes a rainbow, and a cool, peaceful evening time, and songs and drumming around the night fires.

The old Contrary, with his dancing in the thunderstorm, had lifted my frightened heart, too, yet although I think I grasped some of the meaning of his actions as I grew older, I was afraid of lightning until I was sixteen. That summer, while foolishly riding horseback between telephone lines in a dry electrical storm, an earth-shaking violet bolt jumped from the high wires to my arm and down the reins to the horse's withers, burning a narrow strip down the foreleg to the ground. My left arm was numb and paralyzed for a day or so, but it recovered. Curiously, all my fear of lightning went in that one flash, almost as though the stupid ride between telephone lines had been my *heyoka* dance. One could wish that the special wisdom of the Contraries came as easily.

A New One Is Born

෨ BY THE TIME I WAS SEVEN OR EIGHT I HAD begun to sense a special kind of individual responsibility among the Sioux, not only for oneself but for the family, the band, the whole tribe. Then one morning I saw something of the start of this. A small girl from the camp across the road came tapping shyly at our door, motioning to me.

"Ahh, I have a brother too now," she whispered, her dark eyes on the baby astride my hip. "He is just born."

I pushed the oatmeal back on the stove, glanced toward the stable where Mother was milking our cow and hurried across the road as fast as I could, my brother bobbing on my side. I slowed up at the smoky old canvas tipi, shy, too, now, but I did peer into the dusky interior where an Indian woman bent over the new baby on her lap. At the noise of our excitement, the tiny red-brown face began to pucker up tighter, but the mother caught the little nose gently between her thumb and forefinger and with her palm over the mouth, stopped the crying. When the baby began to twist for breath, she let go a little, but only a little, and at the first sign of another cry, she shut off the air again, crooning a soft little song as she did this, a growing song of the Plains Indians, to make the boy straight-limbed and strong of body and heart as the grandson of Bad Arm must be.

I watched the mother enviously. Our babies always cried, and so I had to ride them on my hip, but I knew that none of our small Indian friends made more than a whimper at the greatest hurt, even falling from the high limb of a tree. Now I saw what an old woman had tried to explain to me. During the newborn minutes, that newborn hour, Indian children, boy and girl, were taught the first and greatest lesson of their lives: that no one could be permitted to endanger the people by even one cry to guide a roving enemy to the village or to spoil a hunt that could mean the loss of the winter meat for a whole band or even a small tribe. In return the child would soon discover that all the community felt an equal responsibility toward him.

Every fire became like that of his parents, welcoming the exploring, the sleepy or injured toddler. Every pot would have a little extra for a hungry boy, and every ear was open to young sorrow, young joys and aspirations. I also knew that never, in the natural events of this small boy's life, would he be touched by a punishing adult hand. If he grew up like the Sioux of the old hunting days he would be made equal to the demands of his expanding world without any physical restriction beyond the confines of the cradleboard. I still remember the closed, distant faces of the Sioux when I was whipped for staying out to watch the *heyoka* in the thunderstorm, and at other whippings as well.

The American Indian considered the whites a brutal people who treated their children like enemies—playthings, too, coddling them like pampered pets or fragile toys, but underneath like enemies to be restrained, bribed, spied on and punished, or as objects of competition between the parents, sometimes even to open quarrelings and worse over them. The Indians believed that children so treated could only grow up dependent and immature pets and toys, but with adult wills and appetites to be indulged—grow up designing, angered and dangerous enemies within the family circle, to be appeased and fought and be defeated by, perhaps even murdered. The Indians pointed to the increasing lawlessness and violence of the young people of the white man, a violence that was often turned against their elders. Such a thing was unknown among the tribes in the old days and very rare up to the recent expropriating days, when so many thousands of Indians were driven off their small holdings on the reservations into an alien society. Usually untrained and perhaps practically illiterate, they have drifted into hopeless tent and shack communities around the small towns and to the slums of cities like Chicago, with very few jobs open to them anywhere—nothing much but begging, thievery and prostitution, their white contacts too frequently the lawless and the violent.

His Second Parents

ॐ IN THE OLD DAYS OUR SIOUX NEIGHBORS STILL
had their traditional set of precautions against im-
maturities and resentments among their young people. They avoided overprotecting the young and
saved the eldest son from the mother's favoritism
that could destroy the parents as well as the boy.
By custom every son and daughter, too, was provided with a second father and mother at birth—
usually friends of the blood parents, or some relatives outside of the immediate family. The second
father of a boy was often selected partly for excel-
lence as hunter, warrior, horse catcher, band historian, holy man who listened and advised, or
medicine man—either healer or one learned in rites
and ceremonials. Still earlier the man might have
been a maker of arrows, spears or shields, an outstanding runner or gifted in decoying and snaring
animals. His wife, the second mother, was prefer-

ably known as warmhearted, and fond of boys around the tipi, the lodge. Sometimes the youth showed a special and unexpected talent as he grew and then a third father might be selected, one gifted in this new bent. Or if the puberty dream was of thunder, a *heyoka* might be added as a sort of uncle.

The second mother took over much of the small boy's care so he would never shame his blood mother by trailing at her moccasin heel, never bring the scornful whisper, "Little husband! Little husband!" as he usurped another's place in her attention and affection. The Indians understood the anger and resentment that could grow up in the most tolerant, fortitudinous man if his wife preferred the son over the husband, used the boy against him, brought him humiliation in the village circle. They wanted to avoid the retarded infantilism, the jealousy of the mother, the boy's inability to be a good brother to his sisters and to other girls and women, and finally a good husband and father.

In the second mother's lodge the boy could tease and laugh in a way improper in his own home. He could talk freely, so long as it was respectful. He never used profanity, however, for the Sioux language had no such words, and no obscenities except that practically any word could be made obscene by gross exaggeration. Sex was not a thing of shame or for snickers and embarrassment, although in a prolonged battle Sioux women sometimes taunted enemy warriors with gestures and shouted words indicating they were not men fit for the women of the Sioux.

And when a boy like Young One across the road went to war, whether in the old days against the Pawnees or the Crows, or later, to the Pacific or Korea, the women of his second home could show emotion and cry out, "Be careful, our brother!" and "Be careful, our son!" His blood mother could only stand off and sing the brave heart song for him. I saw this done as late as World War II, while an old holy man made medicine up on a hill for the safe return of these modern warriors of the Sioux.

I recall seeing the second father of the new baby across the road that first day, his white teeth shining in the sun with what seemed the same happy pride as the actual father's. That evening the little group of men smoked in the late sunlight and talked of other days of birth, and how the future was planned then, their words clarified by an occasional bit of sign talk because our father sat among them, passing his sack of Big Bale tobacco around. At the tipis the women bent over the cooking fires, boiling lamb's-quarters and mushrooms they had gathered and frying grouse the men shot that afternoon, with Indian bread, fried, too, and stewed gooseberries from our garden. The blackened coffeepots sent up a fine smell, and blue threads of fire smoke trailed off into the sunlight above the shadowing river valley.

In June a bad hailstorm up on Pine Ridge Reservation in South Dakota pounded the poor little corn patches and the gardens in the creek bends into the earth, so these friends returned to our region and stayed around most of the summer, until potato-picking time in October to make a little cash money. For a couple of weeks the wagons were gone from across the road and the nights seemed empty without the pleasant, nostalgic drumming of Bad Arm as he "threw his mind back" to the old days of his youth along the Powder River and the Tongue and the Rosebud. The Indians had pushed into the sand hills to gather chokecherries, sand cherries and wild plums. They picked up all the game they could find, too, the extra meat to be dried for winter, even if it was jackrabbit, snared and trapped because cartridges were very scarce. Rabbit was not the sweet, fat buffalo that once bulged the folding painted parfleche cases with enough dried meat to carry the Indians through the longest winter. Fall would bring ducks and geese but rabbit was available in the hot, drying time of summer and would taste pretty good boiled with prairie onion in the kettle those months when the blizzard roared around their reservation shacks and the teeth got long and the belly lean.

The women roasted some of the dried meat and pounded it with chokecherries and then stuffed this *wasna*, this pemmican, hot, into flour-sack casings instead of the buffalo bladders of the old days. It was a fine concentrated food, gritty to the teeth from the crushed chokecherry pits but enriched by the nutty taste of the kernels and pleasing to the old-timers like Contrary, whose swollen eyes watered a little in remembering.

By the time Young One was six weeks old he

was little trouble to anyone, either in the cradleboard propped against a tipi pole or riding a
mother's back while she went about her work. He
would be up there some of the time until he was
a year old or more, out of harm's way, seeing all
the world from the high place and unpossessed by
the mother's eyes. Before Young One was two
months old it was decided he must swim, "before
he forget it," the older mother told us, by signs. I
took my baby brother down to see this. The woman
carried Young One into a quieter spot along the
riverbank and with her hands under the chest and
belly, she eased the boy into the shallow, tepid
water until it came up around him. Then, suddenly, his sturdy legs began to kick and his arms
to flail out. The next time he lasted a little longer,
and by the third or fourth time the woman could
take her hands away for a bit while he held his
head up and dog paddled for himself.

Winter babies, boys or girls, who couldn't be
taught to swim early, were thrown into ponds or
river holes in the spring by the father, the impact
calculated to revive the fading urge to swim. Every
Indian child had to keep himself afloat awhile if
he slipped off into deep water, was caught in a

cloudburst or in a river accident while the people were fleeing from enemies or a buffalo stampede.

The young Indian learned to make his own decisions, take the responsibility for his actions at an incredibly early age. When the baby began to crawl no one cried, "No, no!" and dragged him back from the enticing red of the tipi fire coals. Instead, his mother or anyone near watched only that he did not burn up. "One must learn from the bite of the fire to let it alone," he was told when he jerked his hand back, whimpering a little, and with tear-wet face brought his burnt finger to whoever was near for the soothing. The boy's eyes would not turn in anger toward the mother or other grownup who might have pulled him back, frustrated his natural desire to test, to explore. His anger was against the pretty coals, plainly the source of his pain. He would creep back another time but more warily, and soon he would discover where warmth became burning.

The horse dance, by the Horse Society or Cult of horse medicine dreamers, the organization apparently an outgrowth of the old Horse Owners Society, formed when horses were rare and of special powers and responsibilities in war and the hunts.

A Part of His Village

&~ FROM BIRTH THE YOUNG SIOUX WAS IN THE midst of the adult world. There was only one room in the lodge, and only one out-of-doors. Back when he was small his cradleboard often hung on a tipi pole or a meat rack, the wind swaying him drowsily, while the children played and raced and sang around him and one of his mothers or frequently several women worked nearby, busy with the meat or the hides or perhaps beading the regalia of the men.

But the little Sioux had to learn some use of his legs this summer. He spent more and more time on the ground, perhaps on a robe or soft grass but often alone, free to discover his body now and begin to get his discipline in the natural way, as he must be free to take his ideals and aspirations from the precepts and examples of those around him.

When the thrust of the boy's growing legs

took on insistence, one of the fathers or perhaps an uncle lay on his back and held the baby erect for a short walk up his stomach and chest, laughing hard at the sturdy push of the legs, shouting that this was a warrior son, this was a great and powerful hunter. Perhaps the man was a young war chief, or, if older, just out of the evening council circle where any toddler could approach the headmen unhindered. He could see them smoking quietly, deliberating the common problems of today and tomorrow or planning ceremonials and hunts, perhaps selecting the warrior society to police the village for the next moon, and protect it from disturbances inside and out. The boy could hear the crier, always some old and very judicious and respected man, hurry through the camp with any news or with warnings of danger, or of a hunt coming up, perhaps carrying invitation sticks to a feast or a celebration, or proclaiming the council's decisions. And they were decisions, not orders, for no Sioux could tell anyone what to do. The only position a Sioux inherited was his membership in the tribe. He became a leader, a chief because some were willing to follow him and retained his position only as long as the following remained.

In the old days the small children traveled in their cradleboards or in skin sacks hung to the saddle, with other such sacks containing special belongings—finery and regalia, a hard-to-replace pot, perhaps, and seasoning and medicinal herbs, so many sacks that a woman's horse might look like some short, thick, fruit-hung branch. Older children sometimes rode on the pony drags in willow cages that helped keep them from falling out during naps or in flight from attacking enemies. Often an old man or woman was with them, one too feeble for a long ride on a horse or to run. But now and then even the gentlest travois horse took fright and ran away perhaps at the smell of a mountain lion or the flutter of a white petal blown from a giant thistle poppy, horses being what they are. The travois and its occupants might be scattered over the prairie, the willow cage turned upside down. It was very funny and generally only the women were concerned, the young people and the old men laughing hard to see it, those inside the cage, too, if they weren't hurt too much.

The young Sioux rode early. Sometimes before he could walk he was carried behind his father, clinging to the rawhide string of the man's breechclout. He learned to climb up the foreleg of an old mare like a tree, mounting on the right side as the grown Indians all did, the man with the bow in his left hand when he leaped on, out of the way, and leaving the right hand free to draw the bowstring fast.

In the old days Young One would have watched the war parties depart, the women singing them out upon the prairie, and then saw the men come back, perhaps with some missing, the bereaved keening their sorrow in the night. Afterward there might be a victory dance and feasting, the small boys pushing up among the standing legs to see the honoring, too, and later perhaps noticing the warm glances of the maidens for the young warriors, and laughing, as small boys do. Young One would have heard other exceptional services sung through the village—a successful hunt when meat was scarce, a disease ravaging the people stopped, a treaty made for peace and better times.

His Teachers

ʘ FROM BACK BEFORE HE UNDERSTOOD THE words or the wisdom, the young Sioux heard the hero tales of his people told around the evening fires, but in his early years he learned most from the other children. They took joy in showing him all their knowledge, and in practicing the latent parent lying deep in everyone, eager to care for any small creature or being around. But he learned much, perhaps most, from the scorn and laughter of these peers, and from another boy's fist in his face. Eventually he discovered how to avoid some of the laughing, and the blows, or to fend them off.

When Bad Arm, the man who had once carried me home from the plum thicket, was asked if there wasn't injustice in this discipline by children he drew on his old pipe awhile. All life was injustice, he thought. Lightning found the good man and the bad; sickness carried no respect for virtue, and luck flitted around like the spring but-terfly. "It is good to learn this in the days of the mother's milk. Discipline from the young comes as from the earth and is accepted like hunger and weariness and the bite of winter cold. Coming so, it hatches no anger against the grown-up ones, no anger and hatred to sit in the heart like an arrow pointed to shoot both ways."

I remembered what the Young One would learn soon—that his grandfather, Bad Arm, was from the finest of Sioux lines, the old Man, Afraid of His Horse people, prominent long before the

MAN, AFRAID OF HIS HORSE, attacking a Crow Indian, the encounter not in a formal war party; the horse's tail is not tied up.

Indians had horses, when the family was headed
by Man (the Enemy Is Even) Afraid of His Dog,
the *dog* changed to *horse* later, perhaps because the
new creature was called *big-dog* when it became
the warrior's accompanying animal. The Man,
Afraid name was handed down clear into the reservation days by songs through the village when a
son or a nephew grew into the proper character and
prominence. This line has been called the Adams
family of the American Indian, brave and wise in
war and in the council, peaceful, judicious and re-
sponsible, modest and incorruptible. Back in 1854
Man, Afraid of His Horse was asked to become the
head chief for the whites after Lieutenant Grattan
turned his cannon on the government-elevated Con-
quering Bear, whose death scaffold had stood on our
home place for many years afterward, the Indians
told us. Man, Afraid was promised fine presents and
great power, but he told the government men sternly
that the Sioux had no head chief. Instead, there was
a council of headmen selected for regular, specified
terms by the people, who retained the right to throw
them one or all from their high place at any time.
The white man's presents and power were not for
him. Ruefully he reminded them that the man they
killed had been in their high position barely three

years. "It seems that the whites grow tired of their chiefs very quickly."

So the young Sioux learned from his peers, learned from their companionship, their goodness and the power of their ridicule, the same ridicule he saw used against those in highest position sometimes, for even great war leaders bowed in humiliation before concentrated laughter. And he saw men and women of his people walk in dignity through the village circle, the peaceful, orderly village where normally one heard no quarreling in tipi or outside, none except after the white man's firewater came. In the old days the wiser chiefs kept the whisky wagons out of their camps and took their young warriors away from the white man's trails, from the trading posts. The occasional unruly youth or older one was called aside by some well-respected man, perhaps from the troublemaker's warrior society. The next time there was public ridicule, particularly from the women and girls and often from the Contraries. If necessary a humiliating lash of the bow across the shoulders was administered by the village police for all to see. Next his lodge might be torn down, and finally there was ostracism for a year or two, even as many as four. The driving out was done formally, by decision of the council, the man escorted to the edge of the village with his lodge, if he had one, and his other goods loaded on the poles and dragged by an old horse. Anybody who wished could follow the ostracized one, and sometimes several did, even many—enough to start a new camp, particularly if the verdict seemed unjust. But if there was only one man and perhaps his family he went in great danger, for the tracks of a lone traveler, a lone tipi apparently wandering were soon stalked by enemies for the easy scalps, easy horses and weapons that would bring no reprisals. In any case the ostracism was a sad thing, a community failure, and often the women keened as for a death while the driven-out departed and grew small on the prairie.

"It is better to use ridicule early—to keep the young on the good road," Bad Arm and the *heyoka* agreed, telling me that in this, had I been a Sioux, I should have had a real place, for ridicule from the girls and the women stings like the yellow-striped hornet.

In the old buffalo days the very young Sioux learned to snare and track small animals, even the rabbit, with his trick of doubling back on his trail, teaching the hunter to use his eyes while other creatures taught him to sharpen his nose and his ears. As the boy grew he was drawn into the hunting games as he was those of the village: prairie ball, running and jumping contests, tag, snow snake in the winter, and always wrestling and horse racing, the boys riding sometimes so small they seemed like some four-footed creature clinging to the mane and back. Young One would have seen the men pile their wagers in goods at the betting stake before the horses were whipped home with dust and whooping. He would have learned to ride in a dead run while hanging to the far side of his pony with a moccasin toe over the back, a hand twisted into the mane, ready for war. He would have been along on raids against enemy horse herds as a young white man might study his father's methods raiding a competitor's customers.

As the boy grew he ran with his village kind as young antelope run together. He teased the girls, grabbed bits of meat from the drying racks when he was hungry. He went to watch the older youths and young men stand in their courting blankets at this tipi or that one for a few words with the young daughter and could hardly wait until he, too, was a man. He imitated the warriors and ran their errands, hoping to be asked out on a raid, as was done for promising boys, particularly by the war society of a father or an uncle, much as a white youth would be eased toward his father's fraternity, and often with little more bloodshed. Except in a few tribal struggles for hunting grounds, Plains Indian fights were scarcely more dangerous than a hard-fought football game. The first-class coup—striking an enemy with the hand, the bow or the coup stick without harming him—was the highest war achievement, more important than any scalp.

Occasionally the boy was taken out on night guard of the village and the horse herds, or to scout the region for unauthorized war parties trying to slip away, endangering themselves and perhaps the village with avenging attacks. An Indian who gave up the right to cry at birth because it would bring enemies upon the people must not do the same thing by rash and foolish acts later.

Understanding of the regular ceremonials and rituals came gradually to the young Sioux. Eventually he realized what old Contrary told us through the interpretation of his teenage granddaughter, who cheerfully turned all the *heyoka* said around to its rightful meaning. The Sioux camp of any size was always set in a circle because all sacred things were round—the sun, the moon, the earth horizon, as one could plainly see. Even the tipis were round, and their openings as well as that of the whole camp always faced the east, to welcome and honor the light that brought the day and the spring-time. But the simplest and perhaps the most profound ritual that the young Sioux saw was the most common. The first puff of the pipe at a smoking and the first morsel of food at a meal were always offered to the Great Powers—the earth, the sky and the four directions, which included every-thing that lay within their arms. All things were a part of these Powers, brothers in them, and any-one could understand what a brother was.

The Man Within the Youth

ဇ်**&** A**FTER** **HIS** **SEVENTH** **BIRTHDAY** **THE** **SIOUX**
boy never addressed his blood mother or sister directly again, speaking to them only through a third
person. When he showed signs of coming manhood
he was prepared for his puberty fasting by men
close to the family, including some wise and holy
one. There were also holy women among the
Sioux, advising and officiating in many of the rites
with both men and women but not for the puberty
fasting, which was the youth's orientation into
maleness. When he was ready the boy was escorted
to some far barren hill and left there in breechclout and moccasins against the sun of day, the
cold of night, without food or water. The ordeal
was to strip away every superficiality, all the things
of the flesh, to prepare for a dreaming, a vision from
the Powers. Usually by the third or fourth day the
youth had dreamed and was brought down, gaunt

and weak. He was given a few drops of water at a time and some food, but slowly, and after he was restored a little, and bathed and feasted, his advisors and the holy man tried to interpret the vision that was to guide him in this manhood he was now entering.

It was the puberty dreaming of the Sioux war chief, Crazy Horse, that predicted he would not die of a bullet, but that he must always walk as the plainest, the most modest of his people, without paint or war bonnet, without dance or song or voice lifted in the council. Years later, when he was made a Shirtwearer, the highest honor possible, he took the further vow of selfless dedication to the people. Always it was their good that must come first. Now he would walk not only in plainness but the poorest of the poor, his heart turned from the seductions of personal gain and possessions, his ear closed alike to praise, ridicule or any abuse.

"If a dog lift his leg to my lodge, I will not see it," he vowed.

In spite of this dedication Crazy Horse later ran away with another man's wife, the girl he had courted in his youth but as a maiden she had been obliged to bring a man of greater importance, of more mature stature than a young warrior, into her family. Yet after faithful wifehood for some years, a Sioux woman was free to leave her husband, frankly and openly, and the husband, if a proper one, treated her decision with fortitude and composure. Unfortunately this husband was not such a man. He came roaring after the wife with a pistol and shot Crazy Horse in the face. The powder had been split in the cartridge, to supply two, and the bullet only knocked the chief into temporary unconsciousness.

The bullet, however, was powerful enough to split the Oglala division of the Sioux like a rock is split, and because Crazy Horse, by his impulsive act, had caused this, had placed his happiness above the common good, as no Shirtwearer can ever do, he was unshirted. He gave the woman back, and peace was made, yet the Sioux who camped across the road from us still carried the scars of that angry time, as Crazy Horse carried the actual scar of the husband's bullet to the grave.

THE FREE WALKERS

A SOCIETY THAT HAS NO LOCKS CAN TOLERATE
no thief; without paper or other easy record
of man's word it can tolerate no liar, and no troublemaker if there is no jail, no prison. Such a society must orient its young very early. If, in addition, there is no established creed, no organized
priesthood, no one to say what must be believed,
or to offer a refuge, then the members of that society must be given a strong sense of their inalien-
ability from the things of the earth and the sky and
all that lies between. This sense must not be that
of the infant, to whom all things are joined, his to
command, but that of the adult, upon whose conduct all things are dependent. When men are not
brave the rains fail for all, and when the women
lose their virtue the buffalo do not return.

When the puberty rites were over, the young

Sioux had certain duties to perform. With these fulfilled, and the gift of self-discipline, fostered ever since that first suppression of his birth cries, he was perhaps the world's freest man. His first obligation was, naturally, to the family—to help protect and defend the lodge and all its occupants, protect the hunting grounds, help with the meat and with the increase and care of the horse herds, and to bring no discredit upon the good name. He had similar duties toward his village and his tribe. If he dispatched all these he was free to do with his life as he wished, and with no social or economic barriers to any calling, none but inclination and ability. Energy, wisdom and leadership could carry any Sioux to the highest council circles of the village and the tribe, although in years of army pursuit the war leader's chances were the best, as is true in any people.

The youth might decide to work for leadership in a warrior society, hoping for a war chieftainship later. He might be a warrior as most young Sioux were but excel in another field—as hunter, horse catcher or band historian who recorded the events by pictures on skins, later in account books captured in raids or in war, as those taken in the

Custer fight. Now and then a young Indian, usually the son of a holy man, worked to become one, too, one of the modest, listening kind, often with true psychological, religious and philosophical insight. Perhaps he preferred to be a medicine man, either a healer or one who dealt in the mysteries of the Great Powers and directed the rites and ceremonials that were his by vision and talent.

Most of the youths gravitated to the lodges of the warrior societies. These fraternal groups, with lodges in various bands, were usually tribe-wide in membership, or wider. The Dog Soldiers, for ex-

Sioux sabering a Pawnee, identified by the Pawnee roach.

ample, were prominent among both the Cheyennes and the southern divisions of the western Sioux. Usually women did not enter a warrior lodge although each society generally had honored virgins for their ceremonials, replaced as fast as the girls married, or, as rarely happened, one was successfully challenged by some man who claimed he had lain with her in the grass. If the man failed to prove the occasion his property was destroyed and he was driven out of the village.

Some of the members lived at the warrior society lodges, supervised by the headmen, called little war chiefs, one or two of whom was always around to keep the high-spirited youths from foolish acts and forays. Many young Sioux left their crowded homes when they became warriors and kept their bed robes in wickiups, low shelters generally of sitting height, made of willows stuck into the ground and bent over, covered with buffalo robes or, later, with canvas or blankets.

Usually the lodge of the war society selected to police the village for that moon, that month, was moved into the center while the others remained in their designated places in the village circle. These less busy lodges became a sort of refuge from the woman-dominated family dwellings, places for man planning, man talk. Not every warrior belonged to a society; many prominent Sioux, even some powerful chiefs, never did, but they were often temporary guests of one group or another, in their home village or elsewhere. Our old friend, the Contrary, who had to go into a fight backward, had met his wife while visiting at a neighboring war lodge. She was one of the society's virgins, and a warrior brother had to help with the courting for, according to Contrary's puberty dreaming, he could make no affirmative statement that he intended so. He had to say "I do not want you," which offended the pretty young girl even though she understood the general *heyoka* necessity of going backward. It was said that she developed into a very humorous woman, which must have helped in the long marriage.

The food for the warrior lodges was usually prepared and set down at the entrance by women who were either relatives or wives of the members. In a few cases they had to be women with no relatives alive—Lone Ones, as they were called, with all the war society their sons. Sometimes after a victory in a fight or a sturdy defense of the village under attack, a formal feast was carried to the warrior lodge by an adorned and painted little parade, with drumming and songs to honor the members particularly outstanding in the exploit.

The Hunter

&~ THE SIOUX BOY HUNTED FROM HIS FOURTH
or fifth year, first with a rabbit bow his second
father might have made, and wooden arrows, the
points hardened over the coals. Later he got a larger
bow, strong enough to kill a deer or an antelope
with a lucky shot out on the prairie if the young
hunter learned to creep upwind, slowly, with no
more stirring than a bull snake easing up on a
gopher in the grass. And if the young arm was
growing particularly powerful and a pride to the
owner, he might someday be one of those rare bow-
men who could ride up on the biggest buffalo bull
and drive an arrow clear through, to stick in the
earth on the other side, bloody and quivering a little. There are stories of men who did this afoot in
the old days, with the stone-headed arrows, but
they must have been few. Usually the finest hunters were men of patience, guile and speed rather

PLAINS INDIAN HUNTING, before the white man brought guns.

than of power. The exceptionally strong bowman's arm was seldom important except in the surrounds when a bull must be killed, either because he charged, was breaking from the herd or when heavy hide was particularly needed for war-moccasin soles or for shields. The war shields were made of the thick shoulder and hump hide of the bull, the green skin laid over a pit of coals to shrink and harden until it turned an arrow or spear and often a bullet if it struck at an angle.

Feeding a village in the bow days, without the horse, demanded constant vigilance for any game, small as well as large. Even by the cleverest approach, usually only one or two buffalo could be taken before the herd was up, tails in the air, their heavy gallop shaking the ground. Often they stampeded before one arrow could reach them, warned by the sharp-eyed wolves that followed the herds or by the hoarse squawk of the alert raven or the noisy grackles and other birds that rode the backs of the animals to pick insects from the heavy wool.

Without a good buffalo harvest the Indians had to keep hunting all the snowy months, trying to locate what were called moose yards in sheltered mountain foothill pockets or in other broken country. Here elk, deer and moose packed close together and kept moving to trample the snow down while outside it piled shoulder deep or deeper. These animals could be approached upwind on snowshoes and killed as they plunged in panic out into the drifts, perhaps by a knife slash to the throat, the snow suddenly dark with the gushing blood. But moose yards on the prairie, even without moose, were very scarce, and the buffalo scattered in the winter, grazing on wind-swept ridges, hard to find with their wool often snow-matted, the animals gaunted and wild, practically untakable by spear and arrow. The Indian, to survive, had to make big kills in the summer, the meat dried and stored.

Before the horse the Indians sought out sheer dropoffs like those up near Cabin Creek on the

Yellowstone, on the Chugwater of Wyoming or along the White River bluffs. With everybody, including the women and children, helping and, if the wind was right, using fire, a herd might be stampeded and sent plunging over the bluffs, to be finished off and butchered at the foot. But this required an exceptional combination of luck, vigilance and courage. Sometimes the Indians dug buffalo pits to serve as bluffs for the drive.

Even after the horse arrived lone buffalo were killed wherever they were found, with at least two big hunts a year to supply the village through the winter. The fall hunt was for the heavily furred robes against the blizzard winds and for the beds and winter lodge floors and linings, in addition to the fat meat and the tallow. But the fall nights were cool and damp, the meat dried slowly, even during the Indian-summer days. In a July hunt the jerky hardened fast and sweet in a few hours of hot wind, and the hides were easily cleared of their thin summer wool for lodge skins, saddlebags, shield and regalia cases, travois skins and a dozen other purposes. For these, young cows were selected, the skins lighter, thinner, softer and easier to tan and handle, the meat better, too, tender and fat veined.

In the Buffalo Surround

༄ THE SUMMER HUNT WAS PLANNED RIGHT after the sun dance. A few honored hunters were selected to shoot for the old, the crippled, the blind and the sick, while the hunt camp got ready to start at the signal that a good herd had been located. When the successful messengers were brought in and feasted, the hunters started, well organized and disciplined so no overeager one could get out ahead and scare the buffalo, endangering the food supply and the shelter replacement of the people. Even so, a reliable boy or two might be taken along, perhaps with a father or an elder brother, for how was a youth to learn to control his excitement but by practice?

The hunting camp stopped behind some ridge or hill downwind from the herd so no man smell reached the keen-nosed buffalo whose weak eyes were so deep under the mat of forehead wool that

they depended on their noses almost entirely, feeding into the wind for warnings of danger. Even
after the Indians had guns most of the big hunts
were by arrow, safer than bullets flying in a sur-
round and cheaper, with the sale of ammunition as
well as arms often under government ban. The
hunters had stripped to breechcloth and moccasin,
bows in hand, quivers at the shoulder, only jaw
ropes on the horses, the ends slipped through the
manes. Ready, they hid around the snuffling, feeding animals. At the signal they charged out, obli-
quely, upon the herd. The buffalo stopped, sniffed,
lifted their tails and in a sudden thunder of hoofs
and dust, started to flee, turned in a little by the
whooping hunters, then closer, circling in a wild
stampede, tighter and tighter together. The bow-
strings twanged, the arrows found the handiest fat
cows or yearlings and any that tried to break from
the circling, the hunters crying their "Yihoo!" as
the animals went down.

Perhaps a horse stepped into a hole, plunging
forward, the man pitched into the mass of buffalo
galloping past. If he could, he was up and running,
too, leaping on behind another hunter or if caught
in the crush of the frantic herd and not trampled

down, he tried to spring to the back of a buffalo and cling to the bucking, twisting animal by the wool of the hump until he could drop off safely or was thrown. Sometimes a wounded animal charged a horse, catching a curved horn in belly or flank while the hunt swept on around them in the dust and the rising stink of fresh blood and gut shots. Sometimes practically all of a small herd was left dead on the prairie, bunched close for easy butchering. If the herd was large, sooner or later they broke, and while the hunters followed to bring down a few of the drags, the old bulls, they soon gave up and turned back to kill any still alive, perhaps staggering to their feet and dangerous for those running in: the women trilling the cries of thankfulness, the men not in the hunt running, too, and the boys and girls and even the small ones. The sun glinted on the long knives as the hides were stripped back from one side of the buffalo and then the other, the meat cut up while the small children ran laughing here and there, or soberly munched bits of the small entrails emptied of most of the contents and touched with a droplet of gall from the knife point.

Toward evening the long line of pack horses came in, the meat folded inside the skins hanging down, the large bones tied on top to be broken later for the sweet marrow. Those who had stayed at the camp had the meat racks ready, and fine beds of coals waiting. If no one had large kettles a few poles would be set up like tripods and emptied buffalo paunches hung from these to receive pieces of liver, lights, sweetbreads, kidneys and other delicacies with water and heated stones thrown in to boil the contents. At the roasting fires fat hump ribs began to pop and snap a little, and later sent up a fine fragrance while the meat workers cut the larger chunks into flat strips thick as the edge of the hand and the girls hung them over the drying racks.

And when the evening smoke was finished and the meat thoroughly cooked, for the Sioux ate his meat well done whenever possible, some young women went around offering choicer pieces to a hunter here, another there, or sent the crier to invite them to their fires. And afterward there were little songs made for the most successful and important of the hunters, perhaps for one who saved a man from a trampled death, and sometimes for a boy or two who had killed his first buffalo and could scarcely make it seem nothing in his choking pride. Then there was a little dancing by those so young they never wearied. The rest slept, with the scouts far out because wolves drawn by the butchering howled the news of a tired and well-fed hunt camp to the far skies.

Later, while the meat dried hard and thin for the winter parfleche cases, the women took the hides to the stream or lake near camp, to be soaked and treated with the hair-slipping preparations. There would be some fine new lodges in the camp eventually, newly painted to show something of the band to which they belonged, say the Red Tops, and with symbols and figures picturing the dreaming and the deeds of the husband living there.

And when the robes were tanned, painted and worked with dyed quills or trade beads, the finest one of all was taken to the top of a hill and left there as a gift of gratitude offered to their brother, the buffalo, because so many of his relations had died to feed his brother, the Indian, who would, in his turn, die and feed the grasses.

Courting the Girls

෧෨ CLOSE AND INTIMATE AS LIFE WAS IN THE lodge and the village, there came a time when the Sioux boy was suddenly struck by a new mystery about the girl down the camp circle or over at the far side. I recall He Dog, brother chieftain and life-time friend of Crazy Horse, the great leader of the Sioux, telling of their first real interest in the maidens of the village. Although both had killed their buffalo and counted coups in battle as boys along on war parties, almost the same day the two were struck with a burning self-consciousness when a girl looked at them. Suddenly they were too bash-ful to go stand at the water path as usual, too tongue-tied to speak to the girls who had been in the games, the swims, the berryings for years, the girls they had teased and shouted to as casually as all the others only a few days ago. Sometimes this bashfulness was so overpowering that the youth could only sit off on some hillside in the darkness blowing his flute of reed or wood or bird-wing bone, the tones soft and melancholy as a mourning dove's. Sometimes the relatives of the girl were not impressed.

"See how the boy is with his sister and the other ones of his home lodge and you can know how the man will be with your daughter," was an old saying among many peoples besides the Plains Sioux.

Overfamiliarity had been discouraged among these people long before the days of the skin lodge of the buffalo plains, where seven to a dozen or more lived close about the winter fire. The father occupied the place of honor at the back, with his regalia hung above and behind him, the boys and youths to his left, as were any men visitors. His wife and other women and girls of the lodge were at his right, with the old woman, the keeper of the entrance in her place at the lodge flap, seeing all who came and went. Such close living demanded either an iron paternal hand, unknown among these Indians, or a well-established pattern of conduct to preserve order and peace during the long, confining months. Even the persistent joking of the

Sioux was a little formal in the lodge, often in the third person, although the hand game, much like the white man's button, button (except that the hands often moved along a pole slung from the tipi supports), could become very boisterous. This was particularly true if some deft-handed youth disposed of the corn kernel or pebble that was the pawn, or added a couple more.

Despite all the precautions, an occasional young Sioux failed to make his way to a genuine manhood. Perhaps through some early weakness, disease or injury he never freed himself from his mother's moccasin heels into true maturity. Any members of Indian society somehow set apart—the blind, the mute, the born cripple, those whose medicine dreams forbade killing, and those bemused, turned inward upon another country—these were all looked upon as possessing some special gift for the preservation of the band, the tribe. The woman-man, the berdache, was also considered of special sensitivities beyond fact and reality. On the agencies he became an intriguer, carrying his fanciful tales from Indians to whites, and back, as in old buffalo days he was a spy and a diviner of the future, particularly of encounters coming with the enemy. Often he was part of the planned attack by a formal war party. The famous Sioux diviner, Pipe, called Pipe Man and Pipe Woman at various times of his life, was sent out before the decoying of Fetterman and his troops to their death up near Fort Phil Kearny, Wyoming, in 1866. When the ambush was ready Pipe was placed on his horse with a thick black skin hood drawn over his head and face to isolate him from all sight and sound of reality and then sent out toward the fort far beyond the ridge. In a short time Pipe returned, say·

WARRIOR FALLING FROM DYING PONY; the accouterments identify the man.

ing he had some soldiers for them. The war leaders scorned the number and sent him out several times more, until he came back saying, "I hold one hundred men in the hands," meaning that many whites would be killed in the attack.

Now the decoying to the ambush was started, and although Fetterman was wiped out that day, there were only eighty-one men, yet the Sioux still call this "The Fight Where the Hundred Were Killed." They did not count the bodies; they saw no need of that. In such foretellings one believed those like Pipe, but not in factual statements, when the truth of accomplished reality was demanded. The white men—officers or Indian agents—never understood this distinction.

Sometimes young white people speak enviously about the suspected sexual license, the sexual anarchy among American Indians. They are always disappointed to hear the purpose of the old woman of the lodge, the place of the virgins in the rites and ceremonials, and the existence of the society of the One Only Ones, made up of older women who had "been with only one man." But most important was the firm belief that when the women lost their virtue the buffalo would disappear, the people starve. To the Sioux not only the honor but the very existence of the tribe lay in the moccasin tracks of their women. Plains Indian society was a matrilinear one. The husband joined the wife's people so if something happened to him as hunter and protector, she and her children would be with relatives, with people who would care for them, care for their own.

Among the Plains Indians courtship was by fairly fixed pattern, as it is in most tight little societies. From the sixth or seventh year the life of the maiden, always public anyway, was under the watchful eye of the old woman of the lodge, considered particularly indispensable where a girl or young woman lived. This Old One was usually nearby all the waking hours, too, perhaps working skins or making moccasins with the other older women or gambling with the plum pits that were tossed in little grass baskets like dice from the cup.

An old woman or two was always out at the water path on pleasant evenings when the youths and young men came strolling by as the girls returned with their waterskins. Some hoped to catch a shy, modest glance from a particular maiden, or to exchange a few bantering words here and there with the bolder girls, perhaps to tease a little or play an Indian trick or two. Sometimes one of the young boys hanging around sent an arrow through a waterskin and then ran shouting at the girl's cry of alarm as water spurted from the holes. Perhaps she pursued the culprit, caught him and rubbed his face in the dirt a little, laughing, too, now.

The gayest time for the boys and youths was usually when the village moved for fresh grass and water, or with the season. The four old pipe bearers always went ahead, deciding the stops for rest, for water and the sleeps, with scouts far out, the warriors riding in front, at the sides and behind the people, directed by the war society selected to guard this move. The women wore their best beading and finery, their horses gay in the handsome saddle trappings, even the travois and their occupants as decorative as possible. And riding all around the traveling village were the boys and youths, racing their horses, standing on them, perhaps, or slipping through under them at top speed, showing off, hoping to win an occasional high, thin song cry of astonishment and approval from behind the slim brown hand of a girl.

The more formal courting was at the evening lodge door, the youth come to stand patiently outside, hoping a certain girl might slip out to be enfolded in his blanket a moment for a little talk, a little joking. But if she was popular there might be half-a-dozen others waiting, too, all taking their chances at a public slight. Later a young man who felt encouraged might tie a fine horse outside the lodge and if it was led away and added to the family herd, he knew his suit met at least a little favor.

Coups in battle not only got a man honors in his warrior society and praise and songs in the victory celebrations but the warm glances of the maidens, and their preference at the lodge door, when others were left standing. Honors in the hunt were also important, and success in horse raids— like a white suitor's job and his bank account to the prospective in-laws. With the white man the economic gain is usually his daughter's, the new young wife's, but in the fur-trade days some of the more mercenary chiefs went to loaf around the fur posts to barter the prettiest maidens to the white traders and later to the soldiers for gifts and whisky for themselves. Often the young women were not consulted at all, but handed over with no thought for their future when the white man finally threw them aside and, as often happened, no Indian would marry them. Sometimes the white men, particularly the French traders, took their breed children away to school, leaving the Indian mothers to perhaps thirty, forty years of sorrowful, lonely and destitute castoff lives in some so-called squaw camp around the forts or later on the agencies. If the women returned to their people out on the buffalo plains they usually had to live in some lone little tipi at the edge of the village, a hanger-on, dependent upon the meat and hides divided with the needy, for in Sioux society so long as there was meat everyone ate. But for these women the meat came without the pride of contribution—a great humiliation.

In the old days the young Sioux who found his first courting gift, the courting horse, accepted, hunted up some elderly person, often an old woman, to trot back and forth in great busyness, making the arrangements which could not be approached directly without danger of losing face. A proper Sioux could not say to his daughter's suitor, "You are not yet the kind of man she deserves"— not without putting a bad face upon the young man, which was unforgivable among the Indians. But he could say something of this to the go-between who was discreet, and yet let the youth discover that he must show more war honors, perhaps, or more prowess in the hunts, obtain more horses to contribute to the family herd as his share of the upkeep. Some young men worked for years to prove themselves.

Marriage

꒰ THE NOTION THAT BRIDES WERE SOLD ROSE primarily out of the unhappy barter of maidens for whisky by some of the less principled Indians, as happens among any people, whatever the color of the skin or the item of trade received. The practice was much commoner among the Missouri River tribes than with the Sioux, who generally kept their young people away from the white men until forced in by starvation and the army. Early accounts of Indian life on the Plains were usually by those with no understanding of the matrilinear pattern, in which the woman's family accepted the new husband as son in place of the boy who would go to his wife's people when he married, or for the son they never had. As the daughter's husband the young man had every right to the affection, the assistance and protection as a son, a brother and a nephew from his new relatives, and to profit from

78

the family prestige and following. In return he was ideally expected to contribute certain ordinary assets: a good name, honorable and agreeable deportment and the proper honors and coups in the hunts and in war. Besides, since the horse herds were practically common family property, and his to use any time, it was considered only just that he make a reasonable contribution there. The young man's ability as a raider and catcher of horses, the chief item of inter-Indian commerce, indicated, with his success as a hunter, the living he could hope to make for his family. To the European who welcomed a dowry with his bride, this custom of the man bringing the dowry seemed very odd and somehow degrading, but, curiously, degrading to the woman.

Sometimes a man already very prominent in his own band brought the new bride to his village, but even chiefs have gone to their wife's people. Young Chief Little Wolf was a headman among his Cheyennes until he married a Sioux woman and moved to her people, where he also became a chief. But these were the exceptions. When the hostile Sioux surrendered they were ordered to take family names for the agency rolls. Unaccustomed to white man ways, they used the mother's, not the father's. Sometimes these stood on the roster for months, even years, before some sharp-eyed clerk caught the error.

"We have seen that the white man makes his women like toys, like pets. Now we see they are possessions, without names of their own," an old chief protested to his agent up in South Dakota. Plainly the Sioux understood the white attitude toward women no better than the white man the Indian's.

The new husband in a good Sioux family took pride in the fine horse his bride rode when the village moved, and in the ceremonial parades—a horse fit to set off her handsome beaded saddle trappings, her dress of beaded doeskin, later of good red or blue flannel, perhaps decorated with some elk teeth and more to come, occasionally as many as a thousand, heavy but suitable for the wife of a really prominent man. At the start, however, a few teeth were sufficient, with some ribbons and beads. Later there might be rings and bracelets and armlets, too, all these except the elk teeth to be obtained by trading horses, robes and furs, or taken from enemy Indians.

Marriage

Before the days of the traders and their whisky wagons in the villages that would tolerate them, a man usually spent all his married years with the people of his first wife, and any position of importance came to him there. Divorce, however, was not uncommon, for no one could hold a Sioux to anything against his, or her, wishes. Divorce was particularly easy for the woman. The tipi, the lodge, was hers and any time she was dissatisfied with the husband she was free to throw his possessions out into the village circle as public notice that she was done with him. All the man could do was pick up his belongings, his bow and arrows, his gun, his shield, his ceremonial regalia, the feathers of his warbonnet perhaps blowing in the wind, and take them to his mother's home or if from another community, take them to a warrior lodge or a temporary wickiup. He could get a go-between to attempt a reconciliation if he wished, at least he could get part of his horses, his dowry, back if the marriage had been a short one.

The discarded husband was expected to preserve an outward calm, no matter how rankled or grieved. The Contrary whose thunder dancing I saw when a child had been divorced by his first

wife and although it had happened fifty years before, in this he was still not a good *heyoka*. He still
could not act the Contrary when anyone, aggra-
vated by his *heyoka* tauntings, made the gestures
of an angry woman flinging her husband's masks
and moccasins out of the lodge door.

Naturally a man could throw his wife away,
too, if she displeased him, but there was a little
more formality involved. Usually he got a giveaway stick, carved to mean a giving, and at the
next dance he threw it at some man who might at
least take care of the hunting and the protection
of the woman against enemies for a while, if the
couple were not interested in marrying. There was
no permanent obligation attached to catching the
giveaway stick, just a temporary one; mostly it was
a public announcement of divorce.

With perhaps some good horses to be returned
to the departing husband, and the implied criti-
cism of all the family, the woman's male relatives
might try persuasion on the husband. At least he
should let her get the divorce. If, however, the
man mistreated his wife, the relatives took quick
action. He was reasoned with, ridiculed and finally
driven out if he persisted. Once a Sioux who mar-

ried a Cheyenne woman and so joined that tribe struck his wife and was killed by her brothers. At a glance this looked serious. A Cheyenne who killed a brother tribesman, even by accident, was subject to ostracism, but the Sioux was a Cheyenne only as long as he was the living husband of a Cheyenne woman. Dead, he was only a bad Sioux. To his blood tribesmen he was not even a Sioux at all but a very bad man, to strike a woman. His blood relatives sat down with the wife's brothers for a pleasant smoke, speaking regretfully over the fact that there were sometimes such men.

As a husband's importance grew he might take a second wife and even a third, particularly on the Plains. The life of a nomadic hunter and warrior was a dangerous one and most dangerous for the young men, lacking experience and yet the most daring, with reputations to be made for advancement in their warrior society, in the community. Indian women naturally lived longer than the men and yet each one must have a hunter, so they doubled up. Usually the second wife was a sister or cousin of the first, to promote friendliness and peace in the lodge. The thoughtful husband consulted his wife before taking a second. Often the wife made the suggestion. A man's growing power and duties brought more visitors from the band, the tribe and from far off, friends and often enemies, too, as peace emissaries and plain visitors, for Indian wars were seldom continuous and almost never all-inclusive. These visitors had to be fed, made comfortable and provided with guest presents when they departed. In addition there were the children to care for, and increasing ceremonial duties as the husband's stature increased. Without one servant or slave on all the Plains, clearly the chiefs needed several wives. Later, during the Plains wars, the ranks of the men, even the older, were decimated and as the surplus of women grew, many old men far past their fighting and best hunting days had three, four or more women in their lodge or in wickiups hastily thrown together, particularly as the troops burned more and more camps and the buffalo skins became scarce.

The Mother-in-Law

ह IN THE OLD DAYS THE YOUNG INDIAN OFTEN had his mother-in-law in his lodge, but whether there or living apart, his relationship with her was most carefully circumscribed. Proper respect demanded that the two never address each other directly, only through a third person. If they met in the village circle or even when they sat across the fire from each other, it was the ultimate in disrespect to let their eyes meet. This held well into the reservation days. I recall a gay, gregarious young Sioux who liked to visit with the mother of his girl as much as he liked taking the girl to picnics and to dances. Their marriage stopped his pleasant, gossipy visits with his new mother-in-law and finally he maneuvered himself into a divorce. The next day he was in the mother's kitchen again, chair tilted back against the wall, passing the time.

Most of the Plains Sioux were a continent

people, at least those of the buffalo ranges. A man who had been with a woman recently was prone to wounding in an unexpected enemy attack, and in battle the arrow and the bullet were drawn to him. The Sioux usually spaced their children so no woman was encumbered with more than one child too small to run if the camp must flee before an enemy or a buffalo stampede. After the Custer battle it became known that one of Sitting Bull's small sons was left behind in the terrified flight of the women when they saw the troops advancing along the ridge beyond the river. There was scorn for the Bull as a thoughtless, a bad husband, to handicap his wife with two children so close together. Later it got out that the two small boys were twins and so one was bound to be a Little Left Behind, but only temporarily.

The Sioux, generally expansive and gregarious as is common with majority peoples, had dozens of societies: warrior; political, as the chiefs' organizations; occupational, the women beadworkers, the arrow makers; and the ritualistic and religious. Then there were many cults, too, perma-

nent and passing. Practically all the societies and
cults had some socializing attached to their rituals
and ceremonials. When the Indians were driven to
the reservations all societies and cults with religious
or political implications were outlawed, including
the songs and the many elaborate and intricate
dances, with serious destruction of the culture and
the meaning of Sioux life. Some small, inconspicu-
ous groups, usually with five, six members each,
survived, and perhaps even took on greater importance. The Elk Cult was made up of dreamers
about elk, the animal supposed to possess special
power over females and adept at stealing them. It
was assumed that the Elk Cult members knew the
weaknesses, the vulnerabilities of women and had
a woman-procuring medicine that required such
ingredients as the white of an elk's eye and an inside gristle of a hind fetlock. This was aided by
the flute and the mirror and by the presence of two
special virgins at the ceremonials. The Elk Cult
grew on the reservations, particularly on the arid,
thin-soiled ones, with very little work for the men,
work worth doing, the councils without meaning
and power. Their occupations, war and hunting,

were gone, the poor existence gained not by the hunter but by the women waiting in line at the agency warehouses for rations and annuities. It was difficult for the men to feel like men.

So the Elk Dreamers danced often and made the woman-tolling medicine.

The Young Woman

&❧ WITH SO MUCH OF THE TRIBAL FUTURE dependent upon the virtue of the women in the old days, their upbringing was managed as carefully as that of their brothers. The newborn daughter found her birth cries shut off, too, and she was given a second father and mother. The blood mother must be spared the uncomfortable sense of competition from her own flesh and blood always there at the fire. The girl must be protected from the mother's resentment as the woman plumpened and slowed, either in later pregnancies or in age, while the quick and slender daughter of her womb flourished and ripened into fresh young beauty, a constant reminder and rebuke before her eyes. A girl of another blood, accepted into the lodge as a second daughter, seemed so much less a thorn in the woman's breast if not actually nurtured to sharpness there.

A Sioux maiden saw modesty, moderation and poised reserve the approved pattern of life all around her. She learned, often very early, that to the Sioux, courtesy is making others feel pleasant and warm as with the sunlight upon them. Face must be saved but first of all the face of others. "If one shames himself by rudeness to you, then you must make yourself seem to deserve it all, and more."

The small girl saw the women manage the life of the lodge in their quiet and gentle way although some Sioux women were good taunters of enemy warriors and of their own if they seemed laggard. There was an occasional scold and shrew among the wives. Generally these appeared around the army posts and on the agencies, probably exasperated by their men always underfoot, loafing in the shade, perhaps sodden or roaring from the whisky within them. Stories tell of the wife of Red Cloud shouting at the old chief in a most unseemly manner, one that would have cost him much of his fine following in the old hunting and warrior days. But agency chiefs such as Red Cloud was in his later years could not be thrown from their high places like those that the Indians selected, nor did they retire when younger men came up. Agency chiefs were replaced only when they lost their usefulness to the white man.

There were some Sioux women in public life —famous healers and herbalists and a few holy ones who sometimes gave advice, mainly about ceremonials and religious duties and personal perplexities. Like the holy men, they were generally good listeners. Much of Sioux healing was by herbs and earths and poultices and by chants and hypnotism. Often a woman was required by the medicine man's healing because health to the Indians seemed a thing of balance, a basic wholeness, and restoring it needed the two halves, the man and a woman helper. Women and girls, too, sometimes made vows of special ordeal or sacrifice in times of sickness, famine or great war danger come upon the people. They fulfilled these in the proper way, perhaps even in the rigors of the sun dance. They held chieftainships when bands lost all their men of leadership stature, as in the great scourges and in the later Sioux wars, when so many good men died. Sitting Bull returned from Canada in 1881 with a couple of women among his chiefs.

The little Sioux girl learned about life, about birth and death as her brother did, in the natural way, long before she realized their full meaning—a realization that came to her gradually, like growth in the sleep of night, without shock or a sense of betrayal by pretty stories and pretenses.

She saw the care of babies as she sat beside the cradleboards playing with her buckskin doll, the hair like that used for the symbolic scalps on the war shirts—from the curly mane of a colt. Cooking, moccasin making, the care of the lodge and the regalia of its men came the same way. She helped with the meat making, the tanning and decoration of the robes. She learned to cherish the quill and bead designs that came down the woman's line, and to work out their variations, their applications. She discovered the place of floral design in Sioux decoration—for those of white blood, full or in part—and preserved the geometric, the figures of men and of animals and birds for the Indian. As her understanding of the dreams and medicine objects of the men of her family grew, the Sioux girl worked the war and ceremonial shirts, the war-bonnets and special regalia with increasing care and reverence.

When war parties went out the young girl stood behind the women making their songs and dances for the strong heart, for hope and for victory. She covered her head with her robe or blanket in the keening for those who did not return, or

those who had to be borne to the tree or the death
scaffold from other dying. She sat with the gossip-
ing women at work or at their gambling. She went
with the berry pickers, the turnip diggers and the
herb gatherers. Evenings she joined the water car-
riers, shy with the boys and young men who
seemed so ordinary during the day and so strange
in the evening sun. She learned to shoot the small
bow of the children and the women, and to carry
a short butcher knife in her belt, ready for work
and for defense if it was needed against enemies
and any who would molest her, for among the
Sioux a woman had the duty of defending herself
at all cost against attack, against any who would
violate the chastity rope of soft doeskin she was
always to wear when away from the lodge. Such
violation was very rare before the whisky days.
Even after that an occasional man never made another such attempt, for the grab at the sharp
butcher knife * was automatic from a woman's
earliest childhood.

---

* When this happened the man was not driven out as
he would otherwise have been but lived alone in a little
wickiup that he hauled on a drag behind an old horse permitted him, always the last of the people, always camped
outside of the lodge circle, with none to speak to him.

Every Sioux maiden went through a puberty ceremony, too. When she returned from the women's retreating lodge after her first menstrual time, the old crier went around the village calling everybody to a feast for the one who had now become a woman. This was the time to show off a daughter in new garments from handsome moccasins to long shell bands hanging from her braids, a new beauty in her demure manner and the paint of a woman.

Friends of the mother came to bathe the daughter, dress her and seat her in the honored place of the lodge usually set up for the purpose, with prominent ones beside her. Here the girl received congratulations, gifts and songs of praise and promise, and an elaborate oration from a wise man of the village, who outlined the duties of a woman of the Sioux. First there was the long harangue on the greatness of the tribe and then about the girl's family and her duties to them, repeating the reminder: the honor of the people lies in the moccasin tracks of the women. "Walk the good road, my daughter, and the buffalo herds wide and dark as cloud shadows moving over the prairie will follow you, the spring full of the yellow calves, the fall earth shaking with the coming of the fat ones, their robes thick and warm as the sun on the lodge door. Be dutiful, respectful, gentle and modest, my daughter. And proud walking. If the pride and the virtue of the women are lost, the spring will come but the buffalo trails will turn to grass. Be strong, with the warm, strong heart of the earth. No people goes down until their women are weak and dishonored, or dead upon the ground. Be strong and sing the strength of the Great Powers within you, and all around you."

Then the feast was brought up and spread at the lodge door: kettles of soup with the big horn spoons; hump rib roasts on wooden platters lined with arrowhead leaves and water cress; bowls of mushrooms and cane shoots and Indian turnips; coffee with the sweet brown lumps deep in the cup and wild fruits—June berries if in season, and chokecherries, plums and grapes, fresh in summer, dried in winter. All were welcomed to come, to eat, while the father and his friends sat in a little circle smoking, as they did for birth, for a son returning from his dreaming, for the daughter today, and for death. Afterward there was a big dance around the fire for the young people, with the drums throbbing, the singers moving forward and back, the dancers circling, their shadows still bobbing and skipping long over the ground behind them after the push of the crowd had drifted away to the sleeping robes.

There would be talk of the feast, the gifts, the maiden and her finery, and which youth or young man she had drawn into the dance circle first, which one the most often. It was noticed how many had come from far villages, to stand among the waiting men and boys, and with them pretend the proper

GRASS DANCE OF THE SIOUX, in which warriors charge

degree of unconcern. They talked and joked a little among themselves but with a watchful eye for a hand, perhaps a certain hand, to beckon them into the dancing and song for a bit, then to fall back for another, as was proper. There must be no undue show of interest or affection to embarrass the on-lookers. Such display was for the moment one stood in the courting robe at the evening lodge door and for the married ones alone at their home fire. Even the return from the dance was casual, often several young people together, the old women of the lodges

the ceremonial dog kettle as they would an enemy.

a few steps behind, perhaps complaining a little among themselves about the late hour and the chill of the night.

As with any young girl, the next few years were a time for gaiety, for serious and moving thoughts. Not for tears: the Sioux woman was not to cry for less than her people going down. It was a busy time with increasing responsibilities to face and new attentions to meet with poise and no outward excitement, like the quiet workings of the earth toward spring. There were the duties of the virgins in the ceremonials and rituals, so the benefits of these would not fail the people, particularly not the help of the greatest, the sun dance, by which the vows made during the year were fulfilled, and a good harvest of buffalo might be assured.

Wifehood

ॐ SOMETIMES A YOUNG COUPLE SLIPPED AWAY together and when they returned they were made welcome and a lodge set up for them, but they knew that this was not the way for those of good family, for those who honored themselves and their people and would not set a bad face upon them. Usually a marriage was a matter of preparation, both for the community and the individuals. When a man married a young girl it was understood that he would give her time to become accustomed to him, to the new way of living, to wifehood. "Approach the maiden as one would approach any shy creature of the earth, gently, slowly, one step at a time, as one approaches a young antelope trembling in a cactus patch, for the shy heart is the same."

Often the young couple took a sort of honeymoon journey, with perhaps four or five friends along, to visit acquaintances or relatives in some far village. Sometimes they went on a small hunting or war party, leaving their homes gaily, everybody out to see the man and his bride riding in the midst of friends, the woman's young face painted and her hair combed as it might be by her good and loving husband all their years together, the part dusted with ocher—sometimes the dried powder of a prairie puffball, or pulverized ocher ore. Perhaps they went against the Pawnees or the Crows in one of those little raids that were mostly show and posturing and not much more dangerous than the white man's collegiate football. The leaders of both sides were usually careful that not too many got hurt for then there would have to be reprisals. These little outings were common even in later marriages, as the time Crazy Horse ran away with No Water's wife, the woman handsome in her whitened deerskin dress heavy with beads, the vermilion bright on her cheeks and the neat part of her hair ochered by the chief.

When a young married couple returned from their trip they settled down with some old person in the lodge, man or woman, a relative if there was one, or a relative of someone else. No old person

was ever left homeless among the Sioux in the buffalo days. Later, when there was so much pursuit
by the army, with no rests, no time to hunt, just
run, run, often the weaker old ones simply rolled
themselves off the travois in some patch of tall grass
so no one would see and need to turn back, endangering himself and the rest. In an hour or two
the old one would be dead, like some gaunt and
gray birdling in the grass. It was almost like an act
of will. Or perhaps it was sorrow over the greatness
of a people gone, so many dead and so many of
their friends, the buffalo.

The custom of an older person in every home
held true far into the reservation period. The young
Sioux couple needed three things to set up house-
keeping: a bed, a cookstove and an old one. There
was a rigid rule for the old person in the young
home: respect your place. "Advice unasked makes
the fire smoke," Contrary's widow said when she
moved in with her granddaughter and the girl's
new husband. I recall the couple coming to camp
at our place for a few days on their honeymoon
journey. As usual there was the wrinkled, calicoed
old woman smoking her little pipe in the back of
the wagon, among the bedding and bundles.

In the days of the spear and the arrow it was necessary for the Indian woman to carry the bundles because the man had to have his weapons, his bow and arrows, in his hand all the time, ready to fight off ambushing enemies or for any game that

SIOUX TRAVEL BEFORE THEY GOT THE HORSE. They often went far, to the buffalo ranges, the dried meat and hides transported by dog pack and travois.

might flush and be gone. The arrogant and superior white traveler, the superficial observer, assumed from this that the Sioux woman was a drudge, the Indian man a lazy dog—but not too lazy to make a living for his people with crude bow and lance for thousands of years, not too lazy to humiliate the United States Army with the only two wipe-outs on its record—at Fort Phil Kearny and on the Little Big Horn. Both were largely Sioux triumphs if one can call these victories triumphs when it seems that not only the Sioux but all the Indians are never to be done paying for their success.

While the white man was calling the Indian woman a drudge, old He Dog, at ninety-two, told me: "It is well to be good to women in the strength of our manhood because we must sit under their hands at both ends of our lives." He Dog was a fighting old hostile who had clung to the orderly way of the wilds until starvation drove the last gaunt stragglers in to the reservation with Crazy Horse. But he was a wise and gentle man and his women made his long, trachoma-blinded old age a good one, as good as possible on a thin, arid strip of poor ground under the hand of a petty political tyrant called an Indian agent.

The Indian and His Universe

ভ্ৰ VERY FEW WHITE MEN TROUBLED TO UNDER-
stand the Indian's notion of the earth and its rela-
tion to man even as real estate or, for that matter,
the varying Indian attitude toward personal property. To the Plains Sioux nothing that was made
less by division could be inherited. A good name,
the art and craft designs of such things as the arrows and the regalia of the men, the patterns for
beading and painting by the women, these were
passed on to the heirs, those of the men to the male
descendants, the women's down the female line.
Everything else was distributed in a Giveaway
Dance after the owner's death. Some special items
went to friends or relatives, but most of the divisi-
ble property was handed to the needy and the sad
and the unlucky, where it lifted the heart and was
of use.

To the Indians, personal ownership of land
was impossible to conceive. Food, arms, clothing,

livestock could be owned, given, sold or destroyed. The tribe or band might give a man the temporary right to tell a particular story, to sing a certain sacred song or guard and carry a ceremonial object, such as the Oglala war lances or an ancient shield. With membership approval a man could sell or bestow his place in a warrior society. This was also true of some of the women's organizations but obviously not of the One Only Ones, or of the secret bead and handcraft society. The right to use these designs belonged to the woman's line, never to be sold or bestowed, but articles adorned with them could become cherished gifts.

Land was something one obviously could not own. It was held for tribal use and for posterity. Sale of land to the Sioux meant sale of the use. When Indians, from Plymouth Rock to Oregon, sold an area they thought of it as a temporary arrangement. When payment ceased, the land returned to the tribe, or so they believed as long as they could. To the Sioux, land, the earth, was revered as the mother force in the Great Powers from whom all things came. Plainly nothing could ever be done to diminish this land, nothing to make it less for all those whose moccasins walked upon it, and for all those whose tracks were still to come.

Whisky and avarice and starvation changed the minds of some of the chiefs, but their hope of this inalienable right to their earth never really died in the Sioux until the Ghost Dance failed, the medicine dancing that was to bring back the buffalo and all the Indian country. The hope, the dream vanished in the roar of the Hotchkiss guns at Wounded Knee, South Dakota, that winter morning in 1890.

Without a written creed or an organized priesthood the religion of any people adapts itself to new regions, new situations, new ways of life rather quickly. Some Indians, like the Pawnees, carried their sacred place, their center of the earth, with them to the Plains, as the white man brought his altar with its cross and the symbols of the blood and the body of Christ into the farthest wilderness. The Plains Sioux, however, had left the concrete symbols of their religion far behind, and carried along only a few remnants of an agrarian worship, such as the fertility rites discernible in the sun dance and bits of the old corn dances. So intellectualized had their religion become for the more selfless leaders that they were sometimes called the Unitarians of the American Indian.

The realization of death came early and naturally to the young Sioux. There was no demonology left among these people, no evil beings or spirits to be appeased or circumvented. Or blamed. If things did not go well it was not due to supernatural spite or anger or temptation but because the individual or the people and their leaders were out of tune with the Great Powers. To discover what must be done someone had to purify himself of the demands of the flesh, of the selfish, either by fasting on a high place in heat or cold, hoping for guidance in a dreaming, or through the mortification of the arrogant flesh in the sun dance. The hope was for a sharper discernment, a clearer understanding of what must be done, a heightened sensitivity to the Indian's universe, his Great Powers, a closer identification and atunement.

The ceremonial high point of the Sioux year was the sun dance, a modified combination of several old, old ceremonials and adapted to Plains life. It was usually performed in late June or early July, to bring plenty of buffalo for the summer hunt and to fulfill the vows offered during some great emergency the past year, perhaps for protection from cholera, smallpox, measles or tuberculosis, all

SMOOTHING THE PLACE, one of several preliminaries to
leads the entry of the mounted warriors who had rescued

the sun dance. The medicine man carrying the scalp pole
comrades under fire.

very fatal to the Indians because they had none of
the white man's inherited tolerance for them. Some
years dancers had vowed "a red blanket spread on
the ground" meaning blood spilled, actual or symbolic, for escape from a great drouth, from some
approaching danger like a vast prairie fire, an over-
whelming army, the power of the white man to
take the Black Hills and, the few years the dance
was allowed on the agencies, against starvation because the rations that were to pay for the land sold
did not come.

The sun dance varied, depending upon the
dreaming and the medicine of the leader and the
vows to be fulfilled, the tests to be endured for future favor and enlightenment, but there was a
basic pattern. The preparation usually covered
eight days with interludes of ceremonials and dancing. The site was selected and a scout sent out to
find a proper cottonwood tree for the sun-dance
pole. The sun lodge, a wide, ring-shaped arbor
without sides, was erected, the top covered with
boughs, pine if possible, to shade the drummers,
the numerous dance helpers and the spectators.
Then a large group, with a leader, the virgins, the
mothers with babies whose ears were to be pierced,

and many others went out to bring in the pole. The tree was cut down with a stone ax in the old way, cleaned of branches to a foot or two above the forked top, trimmed off there and dragged in to the center of the arbor. Fetishes and banners were fastened to the top, including fertility images of a man and a buffalo, tied on usually by a *heyoka,* a Contrary, and the pole lifted erect with old raw-hide ropes.

When the decorated pole was in place the drumming and singing rose for the preliminary dancing and dedication. Finally the ordeal around the pole began. Each man endured his avowed mortification as well as he could. Some dragged buffalo skulls by thongs tied to skewers thrust through the back. Others took the raw-hide thongs through the breast, the ends fastened to the top of the sun-dance pole, the dancers to circle and leap and jerk until the skewers broke the flesh, free. Some danced the sun-gazing ritual, never taking the eye from the sun, as Sitting Bull did in that desperate time of 1876, during the last great sun dance of the Plains, the Teton Sioux together. He finally fell into a trance and, revived, told of dreaming that many soldiers came tumbling into the

Sioux camp. A few days later Custer and his men rode along the ridge of the Little Big Horn and fell there.

The explanations of the ritualistic elements of the sun dance differ, but to the old buffalo hunters uninfluenced by Christian symbolism and the missionary's Bible stories of pagans, demons and evil spirits, the ceremonial was based on the idea that all things come forth in travail. It was so with the buffalo cow producing the yellow calf, the earth breaking as the grass burst forth, the clouds splitting for the rain. Even the tree bled as the bow was cut and the stone as the arrowhead was shaped from its heart.

In such travail the vows were fulfilled for calamities avoided, and visions like that of Sitting Bull, of things to come, were born.

When the last of these stubborn and determined Sioux were finally driven to the reservations every effort was made to break up their ability to protest, all their will to resist. That meant that the tribal organizations and what gave them their unity and power—the Sioux religion which permeated every act of the Indians—had to be destroyed. Most of the ceremonials, all those that could be detected, were stopped, including the sun dance, which had gathered not only the band but the whole tribe in an annual unifying religious ceremonial. It was easy to secure public sentiment for the suppression, not only through the exaggerated reports of the self-torture in the dancing but the whispers of sexual exhibitionism in the little fertility figures tied to the top of the sun dance pole. So, despite the Constitution's guarantee of religious freedom for all in the United States, the sun dance was out-lawed for the Oglala Sioux in 1881 and not re-stored until 1930, "without torture" and in connec-tion with what the old-time westerners called a pop-stand rodeo.

Several of us interested in the Sioux were there to watch the head dancer, seventy-eight, lean and gaunt as any of the buffalo-hunting followers of Crazy Horse out on the Powder River. Dusty in his paint and flapping breechcloth, the old dancer made his slow little jumping, slipping steps, always turned to face the broiling sun as the drum-mers pounded the green calfskin, the voices of singers rising and gone, to rise again. The dancer was supposed to maintain his movement each day from sun to sunset, but on the final afternoon he was beginning to move in a curious trance-like flow, almost without steps. Suddenly he stopped, cried out in a thin, high falsetto, gesturing to his bare breast, crying to the sky and the sun-dance pole and all around.

"He wants the thongs," a uniformed Indian policeman told us, as voices from the headmen replied to the dancer, patient at first, then angrily and with a denying tone, firm. It could not be allowed.

"Not allowed!" an old woman near us exclaimed, the words plainly unfamiliar upon her tongue but their meaning sudden and dark.

For a moment the lean old dancer hung as from a string that did not exist. Then he crumpled down into the dust. A murmur of horror swept the crowd, the eagle-wing fans still. Then there was silence, a naked stillness, the dull drumming and the song vanished, dead.

There was a scrabble of people getting to their feet and four men running out to carry the old dancer away to the sweat lodge, a low wickiup with water to throw on hot stones. An Omaha dancer came out posturing in the buffalo bull's fighting step, to paw the dust and shake his bustle of feathers that switched the old bull tail hanging

from the center. He was followed by others, dancing their special steps, but many faces kept turning
toward the sweat lodge and the men creeping in
and back out. After a while word spread that the
old dancer was alive, sleeping, his four-day ordeal
cut short, finished. But there would be bronco bust-
ing at the rodeo corrals, beginning immediately.
The riding was good, and it seemed that almost no
one remembered, or even knew, that at the sun-
dance pole an old man's moment of hope and belief had come and gone.

The Sioux had two hundred years of contact
with white men who carried the cross with them
in one guise or another and on top of that, eighty-
five years on reservations where churches, Catholic
and Protestant, were pushed, with political favor
for those who joined and a little coffee and perhaps doughnuts for all in the hungriest times. Still
the Indians didn't take Satan and hell-fire very
seriously, or the concept of an avenging God. The
idea of fear was too alien to their philosophy, to
their ideal of personal discipline and their whole
idea of the good life and the eventual death that
comes to all, bitterly resisted or embraced with

grace. There was no fear of the dead among the Sioux. The body of a warrior who fell in enemy country was rescued immediately if possible, or by a later party with the skin sack painted red for the honorable return. Often relatives and friends went to sit at a death scaffold, later at the grave, as they would have gone to the fireside of the departed one. Children saw the sickness, the dying and the burial, and sometimes went along to visit the place of the bones, to listen to the stories of what had been done, and the duties and responsibilities left for those behind. Sometimes there was a song or two, or some grave little dance steps.

The Indians have added much of their own religious concepts to their notion of Christian beliefs and symbols, and, with the peyote trances out of the Southwest, have formed the Native American Church, which, judged good or bad, is their own. But even those who joined the churches of the white man have clung to some of their basic beliefs, which were broad enough to encompass practically any formalized creed. One Sunday morning, while camped along an agency trail, I went out for wash water from the creek. As I stooped to dip it up, I heard low Indian singing and the swish of water below me. A naked young Sioux, glistening wet, knelt among the gray-green willows of the bank washing a blue shirt. I saw him lift it up out of the water toward the sky and then dip it to the earth and all around, as the pipe and food are offered. I slipped away, and a couple of hours later the young man came riding by, wearing the clean blue shirt. He raised his hand in greeting, palm out, in the old, old gesture of friendship—the left hand because it is nearer the heart and has shed no man's blood. He was on his way to mass at the Mission but it could have been to the little Episcopal church on a knoll, with the sermon and the Book of Common Prayer in Sioux, or any of half-a-dozen other churches, wherever his grandparents or his great-grandparents joined when they came in from the buffalo ranges. He was going in a shirt offered in the old way to the Powers of the world, in recognition of his brotherhood in them.

Among the Indians, as among any people, the depth and profundity of religion varied, and varies. There were always some who never rose above attempts to obtain help for selfish, personal ends, but it seems that the average Sioux tried to accept responsibility for what happened to him and his band, his tribe, mystically as well as in visible actuality. When misfortune struck there was no devil to blame. The individual or the group was out of tune with the Indians' universe. Farseeing men went to fast and wait for the vision of what must be done to regain the harmony with all things encompassed by the Great Powers.

"In them all things are one: the rock, the cloud, the tree, the buffalo, the man," Bad Arm used to say, ending with the sign for the All—the flat right hand moving in a horizontal circle, high as the heart.